The Family Enterprise Playbook:

A Framework for Action

By

David C. Wells, Jr.

This book presents the ideas of its author. It is not intended to be a substitute for a consultation with a financial professional. The publisher and the author disclaim liability for any adverse effects resulting directly or indirectly from information contained in this book.

The Family Enterprise Playbook
Copyright © 2023 David C. Wells, Jr.

All right reserved. No part of this book may be reproduced or used in any manner without the prior written permission of the copyright owner, except for the use of brief quotations in a book review.

To request permissions, contact the publisher at info@davidcwellsjr.com

ISBN: 978-1-7356813-3-7
First paperback edition published November 2023

Dedication:

For my parents:
8 and 14-hour car rides to the grandparents every year
did wonders to instill an appreciation
and love for the power of family

Contents

Introduction *7*

Chapter 1 – The Starting Place: What Comes Next? *13*

Chapter 2 – Introducing the Strategic Action Model *21*

Chapter 3 – Family Identity *27*

Chapter 4 – Vision *35*

Chapter 5 – Strategy *39*

Chapter 6 – Implementation *53*

Chapter 7 – Governance *57*

Chapter 8 – Concluding Matters *63*

Appendix *67*

Introduction

"Of making many books there is no end, and much study wearies the body."—Ecclesiastes 12:12

Writing a book, as well as reading one, is not without cost. And so, before starting either (writing or reading), one should consider if the path ahead is likely to be worthwhile.

Let me go first. Does the world really need another book on wealthy families, family businesses, family enterprise, or family offices? Has enough ink been spilled already? Moreover, is there anything new left to say?

These are the questions I asked myself as I sat down to draft the book you have in hand. At the risk of begging the question—the answer I think is yes. I'll tell you why in just a second, but first let's flip the question.

Why are you here? Why pick up this book?

There might be a few different reasons why this book would appeal to you:

- As you arrive in mid-late middle age, you find yourself contemplating your legacy.
- Perhaps you have attained a level of financial success and are now focused/worried/concerned about the effect of this wealth on future generations.
- Finally, you would like to understand how families are able to set themselves up to persist for four-plus generations (around one hundred years).

These are tough questions, and in the face of ambiguity, it is hard to know what to do. The academic community refers to it as "decision-making under uncertainty." The human brain is wired to seek out certainty, and to take all steps possible to attain it—aka—this is challenging stuff.

Ambiguity may seem an odd place to begin a book looking at the family, but it is the exact right place to start. We live in changing times for the concept of family. On the one hand, we likely are all familiar with the ubiquitous statistics around falling birth rates, lower household formations, and high rates of divorce. At first glance, it seems that family might be a concept that has had its day in the sun.

And yet, there are several dynamics at play that are giving the concept of "the family" a new lease on life. Combined with escalating rates of technological change and the shifting sands of geopolitics, today's world feels more uncertain and fragile than ever. Into this space, the certainty of family, even with all its foibles, can feel like an excellent ballast in the storm.

Even more, on the ground, technology has allowed families to stay connected in ways never thought of before. Parents talking with adult children daily. Aunt and uncles on Snapchat and TikTok swapping videos with nieces and nephews. With group text messaging, smart photo albums, and low-cost airfares, families can stay connected like never before.

For many, there is a growing desire to build families who stay relationally engaged for many generations. These "enduring" or "legacy" families have historically been quite rare—names like Rothschild and Rockefeller come to mind. More and more, new families are beginning the journey. It is a fascinating dynamic to watch.

Over the last thirty years or so, academic research, practitioner expertise, and peer experience have combined in a unique way to understand and develop a view of how such families are built. Initially, this was focused on the family-owned business and addressing succession issues that far too often imperiled the business.

Yet as time has passed, additional research and thinking have been added to elucidate how families who are generational in nature have been successful. The thought leaders in this space have defined, in my view, the why and the what—that is, why families might attempt the legacy journey and what successful families are doing.

And yet, how a family, your family for example, might do the same is not always clear.

For the families I work with and have gotten to know over close to twenty years in financial services, **there is a near-universal commonality—a sense of being overwhelmed.**

Far too often families simply do not know where to start. They have read the books, been to the conferences, and spoken with peers—and yet the size and complexity of the matter limit their understanding of how the pieces come together and where the journey begins.

While the books and thinking of the field have tremendous wisdom and insight, they have often come at the cost of simplicity and clarity of action. If you think shopping for toothpaste is overwhelming, the never-ending list of to-dos for a family is just as bad. There are often lists upon lists of possible steps for a family to take, but often without a clear sense of why each activity matters and what sequence to engage in, especially if the family is still small.

This book is an attempt to rise above this well-meaning, but far too often, chaotic fray. **This book outlines a simple framework I have developed that will help you understand the task ahead of you.** With that in place, you can dive deeply into specific questions or activities, but with a clear sense of how they fit together.

The best place to begin when encountering any subject is to have a model of how something works. Once that is in place, then you can build on layers of complexity and nuance. Calculus is great, but not if you have not had pre-algebra first.

A bit of orientation before we get going.

First, the average reader reads 250 words a minute or around 15,000 words an hour. This book has less than 15,000 words—it is meant to be digested in around an hour.

This book is meant to be a guide, a how-to, for the long-term-minded family. It will cover frameworks of action without being overly prescriptive. You know your family best; this is meant to provide the operating system for you as you march through time and space together.

The path to this book began with an inadvertent question I asked myself: namely, if you were to build a one-page dashboard that showed whether a family was on track toward its goals, what would be on that dashboard?

I love the simplicity of dashboards—a quick snapshot that points to organizational health, shows key metrics and goals, and outlines progress toward them. As the saying goes, "What's measured gets managed."

But, as I sat and attempted to draft out a simple dashboard of a legacy-focused family, I was confronted with the reality that I did not fully understand how all the parts of the legacy family work together and if done thoughtfully can create a feedback loop that becomes self-reinforcing.

This study began about a year's journey to dive deep into this question and the model we will discuss, what I call the Family Enterprise Strategic Action Model (or SAM for short).

Chapter 1 – The Starting Place: What Comes Next?

We have, of course, all heard of the proverbial man with the hammer—for whom every problem looks like a nail. In today's world, something that even looks like a nail would be a welcome relief. Said differently, today's problems span many domains and make it near impossible to know what tool we need.

In my experience, wealthy individuals and families share these same dynamics. Knowing what to do with wealth after it arrives is among the most uncertain and complex of questions to wrestle with. This may not appear to be the case at first glance. But consider a few additional dimensions.

When we are children, we often dream of the day when we can afford to buy everything on our wish lists. Come birthdays and Christmas, my own children have running lists of all the possible possessions they can discover that they think will bring them happiness and enjoyment.

Adults are no different, although the numbers involved are simply larger. Yet the reality for most wealthy people is that they can most likely buy anything they would like, when they would like it. Even in today's world where experiences are more in vogue than possessions (and for good reason), there is a finite amount of vacation or pleasure-seeking that someone can engage in.

At some point a wealthy person must realize that there is more than enough capital in the bank. When that occurs, a sober-minded and thoughtful individual *should* pause and consider their affairs as they contemplate their future direction. My first book, *When Anything is Possible*, is addressed to those sitting in that moment and offers a framework for thinking about these nuances.

Now, I said "should"; the reality is that far too often this sort of effort does not occur. This work of self-reflection and discovery can be undertaken at any time. But generally, the earlier, the better, as it provides critical input for what comes next.

For most individuals, the most frequent conversation around wealth deals with risk and liability management, most often through the lens of tax and estate planning. This is an important dynamic and must be done well to see wealth grow over time. The challenge is that as individuals engage in this estate planning work, they inadvertently end up crossing a gate into a new phase of consideration, far too often without being aware that this shift has occurred.

Figure 1 – Phases of Planning

As someone starts estate planning, they believe that they have started a series of conversations that are individual in nature. And while it is true that estate planning is tied to the individual or couple, it is not *only* related to the individual.

The current tax code offers compelling incentives to move assets to future generations of the family—one's children and grandchildren can easily benefit with even simple planning techniques. Planning conversations as a result often move quickly from the individual zone into the family zone, **which may in fact be unfamiliar territory.**

Some families share a story like this: A founder-entrepreneur has a dream to build something, even if that something is just a steady paycheck. **As this dream grows, it may begin to incorporate the broader family**. There may be a desire for or by future generations to work on this dream in full-time employment, aka a family business.

Over time, this dream may expand further for the family to continue to own a business and stay involved in each other's lives in effect for generations, creating a modern-day family "tribe."

But for many other families, there was never a goal to work on a dream as a group. Yet, after financial wealth was created through entrepreneurship or employment, this wealth is put into trusts, foundations, and other planning structures that require group involvement.

These structures allow the family to avoid high levels of estate tax, as well as provide protection against creditors and lawsuits. **But in utilizing these structures, the wealth-creating generation has had an impact on the future generations of the family.** In many cases, this creates work that the family group must engage in going forward—whether they are ready, prepared, or willing.

The family has come to a crossroads and must consider what is the right course of action.

Now that the broader family is affected/benefited/inflicted (depending on their point of view) by the assets of prior generations, a dialogue must begin regarding what the family wants to do in light of this new state of affairs.

They may consider such questions as:
- Is there a need to educate future generations?
- Does the family want to stay together over time?
- If they do not want to stay together, what is the right level of wealth to give to future generations?
- For the assets that are remaining, how should they be deployed to realize the greatest possible value for the wealth-creating generation?

While these questions may seem intimidating, there are a few common options that families choose from as they consider the wealth and the family. For simplicity's sake, let's look at them along a few different dimensions. The first dimension describes where the assets go after the passing of a generation. The second dimension considers the behaviors required by the planning. Some planning allows a beneficiary to be focused solely on individual concerns, while other planning is more collective in nature. The final dimension considers the motivation behind utilizing this option.

Option 1 – Do Nothing for Future Generations
- **What is it?** G1 chooses to give future generations nothing. G1 spends wealth and then gives away the balance to charity.
- **Individual or Collective?** Individual dominates, but only the individual of first generation of family. Limited opportunity for individual value add in future generations.
- **Why Choose this Option?** It is "not our job to provide for future generations" or morally more important to support charity.

Option 2 – Rule from the Grave
- **What is it?** Assets go to future generations but with lots of restrictions/controls.
- **Individual or Collective?** While the assets go to the future generations, all the controls and restrictions limit future individuals by keeping the focus on the prior generation.

- **Why Choose this Option?** "Limit the damage." Don't want to ruin the person from the wealth, can signal low trust in future generations.

Option 3 – Set a "Finish Line"
- **What is it?** G1 defines "enough" and gives set amount.
- **Individual or Collective?** Opportunity for future generations, but nothing collective as "family."
- **Why Choose this Option?** Provide assets to future generations, but put some limits to accomplish other goals (charitable) or avoid doing harm.

Option 4 – Build a Family Enterprise
- **What is it?** Perpetuate the family, a variety of structures.
- **Individual or Collective?** Collective is best served when individuals thrive personally and have desire and opportunity to contribute to the collective.
- **Why Choose this Option?** Creation of a modern-day "tribe."

Option 5 – Family Governance Only
- **What is it?** Many possible choices; some wealth may go to individuals, some to family foundation.
- **Individual or Collective?** Collective first and then some individual.
- **Why Choose this Option?** Growing focus on the family, but often counter-balanced by a family business or even strong patriarch who dominates.

Option 6 – Must Perpetuate Family Business
- **What is it?** Only focus is on perpetuation of the business, any assets used for that goal.

- **Individual or Collective?** Entirely collectively focused, no place for individual.
- **Why Choose this Option?** Goal is to keep business intact, but no place for individuals in family outside of business.

It is helpful to think of these options on a spectrum from entirely individual to entirely collective.

Which then is the best option? There is by no means a universal blanket best option. Generally, I would argue that options three and four are the most preferable in the long term as they have the best odds of leading to a positive outcome.

Under the finish-line approach, prior generations determine how much to give to the next generation but do so with a mentality of creating opportunity for future generations. There are no expectations of staying involved as a broader family in the future. This course of action is for many the most thoughtful and realistic option. If this is the path chosen, the task afterward is to ensure that the family is prepared for the assets that will come after the planning is complete.

For more and more families, the idea of a family enterprise is growing in its appeal. This solution is appealing for many reasons. It enables the family to continue to stay together into the future—providing wonderful continuity in a changing world. A broad view of the family also allows each member and generation to find a way to contribute. This honors and empowers the individual talents that a family member has by giving them a place to be utilized.

Far too often, those without the professional acumen or interest required can feel left out of the family's future path. The family enterprise creates a much broader tent for involvement.

But as we will discuss, this path is not easy and will require the family to grow and evolve in intentional and thoughtful ways. It can be a daunting task, but the stories of families who have made this effort show that it is well worth it.

Suggested Reading:

Tribe by Sebastian Junger

Tribal Leadership: Leveraging Natural Groups to Build a Thriving Organization by Logan, King, and Fischer-Wright

Chapter 2 – Introducing the Strategic Action Model

The remainder of this book is focused on the subset of families who are focused on building a family enterprise. For those of you unfamiliar with the term *family enterprise*, it is an umbrella term that encompasses all various entities a family might develop, including a business, family foundation, family office, family council, and family assembly.

The choice to build a family enterprise should not be made lightly. For a wealth creator, to this point, the family is likely just a social system. It is a network of relationships between them and those with whom they enter into the deepest of human relationships, calling each other family. Families do things like share meals, have holiday traditions, travel together, and tell stories.

But there is a natural gravity to the vast majority of families. As the family grows and expands, the family begins to drift apart. First cousins may know each other, but commonly, second cousins do not. Building a family enterprise must then work against this natural tendency of distance to enter into family relationships.

As we discussed in the chapter prior to this, there may be many tax and estate planning reasons why it makes sense to put financial wealth into trusts, family foundations, and so on that allow wealth to move to many generations into the future. At the same time though, creating these entities also will affect the family relationships themselves.

As such, because the family has a reason to stay together (through the shared ownership of assets) and the ability (through the wealth itself), the family must decide that it wants to stay together relationally.

This shift begins the migration of the family from a social system into a social organization. The great power and opportunity of organizations are their ability to set goals, marshal resources, and achieve an objective. That said, it is highly uncommon for most people to think about their family in these terms. Moreover, and as we will cover in chapter 7, it is atypical to think about a family having any sort of formal governance system.

Thus, while building a family enterprise can be a compelling idea, it is not a panacea. As the work begins to build this entity, all sorts of new strategies, structures, and processes will begin to emerge by necessity. The net result is that there will be a big bang-esque explosion of complexity. There are a lot of moving parts, and over time, this will only grow more and more complicated.

In the face of complexity, it is challenging just to keep abreast of everything that is going on, much less understand the current situation and ensure that everything is marching toward the desired outcome. To that end, various explanatory models have been developed over the last thirty years to help explain and clarify various parts of a family enterprise.

The three circles diagram (only developed in 1978) comes immediately to mind, which discusses different roles that someone may play (family, business, or ownership). Other models have taken a resource-based view (Jay Hughes 5 Capitals concept) or a decision-based view (Banyan's 4 rooms).

George Box wrote, "All models are wrong, but some are useful." No one model can encapsulate all dynamics at play for a family. And while the families I have spent time with often find existing models helpful, far too often, those families often look like the proverbial deer caught in headlights.

While they may be able to use a tool to understand where they are, they are far too often unsure/uncertain/paralyzed about what steps to take to move forward.

Introducing the Strategic Action Model (SAM)

So why is that the case? As I mentioned in the introduction, this confusion arises because families often do not have a clear understanding of how who they are, where they want to go, and what they must do are interconnected and self-reinforcing.

The challenge and opportunity then is to find a way to provide a clear framework so that the family can coordinate its actions and see how the pieces come together. This allows the family to understand what it is doing, why it works, and where potential gaps might be.

To that end, I have spent about a year working on what I have termed the Family Enterprise Strategic Action Model (or "SAM" for short). The model is *strategic* first. It is designed to help the family make the choices necessary to achieve its goals. It is also action-oriented, meaning that it should help you decide what to do next.

While it should not be prescriptive in defining the exact course of action for a family, it should be directionally indicative of what steps to take and when to take them. It should be akin to taking a map and a compass and then knowing roughly which direction to start hiking.

This is not meant to replace existing tools, but hopefully provide an overarching model that allows other tools to be more constructively used to allow specific practices to be thoughtfully deployed. Think of something akin to a blueprint.

Figure 2 – The Strategic Action Model

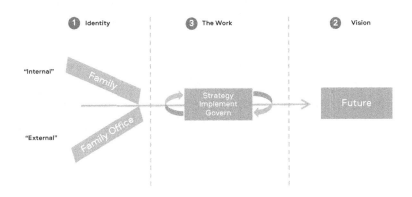

While we will unpack each of the elements in greater detail across the rest of the book, let's quickly review each of the pieces.

First, notice there is a horizontal line in the middle of the model. This line separates things that are internal to the family, aka must be done by the family itself, from things that are external to the family and might be done by a family office, other outside advisors, consultants and/or board members.

Second, there are three phases of the work. The first phase is around the identity of both the family and the service organization (aka family office) that helps the family enterprise function. The second phase deals with vision, where the family enterprise is ultimately heading.

Finally, in the middle is "the work"—that is, the strategy, implementation, and governance of the activities the family enterprise will choose to engage in to achieve its vision.

Each of these elements will be unpacked in much greater detail over the coming pages. Note that this model provides a thirty-thousand-foot view of the family enterprise. At that level, the dividing lines between various entities tend to get blurry; as such this is not necessarily about apportioning power and responsibility, as much as it is about seeing how the parts come together in service of the greater whole.

Chapter 3 – Family Identity

- **Concept - Who Are We?**
- **Capabilities - What Are We Good At?**
- **Capital - What Do We Have?**

Before a family can do anything, it must have a dramatically clear sense of who it is. Wishy-washy platitudes are inadequate. It will be impossible to achieve a long-term, aspirational goal without this in place.

That said, answering this question does not necessarily entail long-form, painful naval gazing. Rather, it involves unpacking a holistic understanding of the family in all its facets. A family with a clear identity has developed and articulated the answers to the following three questions.

Before we jump in, we must consider who is part of the family at this point. Depending on the age of future generations, the family may consist primarily of the wealth creator and spouse. This should be viewed as a starting place. As the children come of age—meaning entering adulthood (18+)—it will be important to loop them into these conversations.

As we discussed in chapter 2, the family enterprise concept is a collective concept. It entails multiple generations being purposefully engaged. As such, you want to build this muscle memory early and often in each generation. Also, by finding ways to involve the next generation early, you give them the opportunity to contribute to the effort—which generates buy-in, in the same way that Ikea has customers assemble their own furniture. There is a profound sense of ownership that emerges when you are involved in building something.

Question 1: Who Are We?

The Oracle at Delphi's maxim to "know thyself" remains a timeless and sacred task for families. Because this is such a big question, it can be helpful to think about it in two parts.

First part—the family needs to have a clearly articulated view about why they want to build a family enterprise and a legacy-focused family. **This articulation must be shared by all family members of adult age, not just the patriarch/matriarch leadership figures.**

A clear articulation is critical as it can be ballast in the storms that are certain to come, and a lighthouse to help orient the family when changing times and circumstances makes it even more difficult to know what direction to head. This *why* can evolve over time; it only needs to be compelling for today.

The second part is an articulated, defined, and agreed-upon set of core values of the family. Values are more than just words like "hard work" or "stewardship." The family must articulate what those words mean in their unique family context.

Then, these words and their definitions must be agreed upon by the family. While it may not need to be unanimous, the family must positively be able to positively agree to the list and say that those terms are an accurate reflection of what they perceive at this time.

While discussing core values, I would offer that if this discussion were not emotional or heated, you are likely not doing it correctly. For the values to be real, they must in fact be something that you value. When you share your values, it should feel vulnerable. And moreover, if there is a difference of view, the intensity of your belief in the value should create the potential for heated dialogue or at the very least, a deep discussion.

This is not to say that the family should plan for an argument, far from it. Instead, there should be a degree of empathy and nuance that each family member brings to the discussion. There is a critical and key difference between the values of the family and your personal core values. While those Venn diagrams may overlap, it may not be complete. The family should be working to articulate what their values are **together**, together being the operative word.

Question 2: What are we good at?

Families who are building for generations must have some core capabilities in place; that is, they must have the skills necessary for the work ahead. **If they do not have them, they must be open to building them.** If they are not open to doing the work/learning required—this is a strong indicator that this path might not be the right one.

To begin, the family must take stock of the current capabilities of the family and their level of development.

For example, the family may think that communication skills are something that should be important to have going forward, and the family may even think that they are good at communication. But when you take stock and ask family members if they feel heard or if they have a venue where they can express a point of view, the reality on the ground may point to something very different.

There are a whole host of additional capabilities that the family will need to have. Consider the following:

- Can we work together? Do we know how to organize ourselves to accomplish a task?
- How are decisions made? How is power exercised within the family? Is this power model durable for the long term?
- Do we know how to take risk, to be entrepreneurial?
- How does the family preserve tradition, but also remain innovative to avoid becoming brittle in a changing world?
- Can we manage conflict? Can the family disagree but remain in relationship?
- Can we manage hardship/suffering? How will we handle the inevitable griefs that come?
- Can we welcome others in? Does every generation onboard both in-laws and the next generation?
- Can we learn? Is the family self-reflective enough to identify knowledge and skill gaps and capable of the learning required to address?
- Does the family have special know-how and skills that can be monetized?

The wise family can both identify its current level of development, as well as understand where they are heading and what capabilities they will need when they get there. At this stage, there is no need to reach judgment about the presence or absence of a capability. It is more important to be aware of the fact, as it will prove a vital input into the strategic planning process to follow.

Question 3: What do we have?

This final question may sound simple, but it is important to not gloss over answering it. Most straightforward is the financial capital of the family. Yet even within something as tangible as dollars and cents are a few additional considerations. For example, how liquid is the financial capital? Overall levels of liquidity will shape the art of the possible in terms of investment choices to hit longer-term goals.

Also consider the ownership structure of the assets. This would include assets held directly by family members and would determine who calls the shots. Over time, for many families, most of the assets are held in trust. Trusts are typically used for long-term estate planning assumptions. But in those cases, who the trustee is, and their risk appetite will affect the complexion of the investment assets.

The second main bucket of assets is the human capital of the family. There are lots of different definitions of "human" capital. Some are more expansive in nature, and others are more specific.

But what I see in the marketplace is a lack of consensus around the definition. For our purposes, I think it is easiest to think of human capital as the actual family members themselves. The professional talents, relationships, and know-how of the family are a tremendous asset to the family.

This is different from the capabilities of the family because it focuses more on the family; that is, does the family consist of and continue to produce healthy human beings who are ready to contribute to the overall well-being of the family? Are there unique skills, abilities, and interests that can be deployed to help the family? Are we able to systematically capture this information to deploy human resources when an opportunity presents itself?

Conclusion

The family's core identity (and values), capabilities, and capitals are just the ingredients that will be utilized over time. The next critical element is a vision, which we will cover in the following chapter.

Suggested Reading:

Family Wealth by James E. Hughes

Borrowed From Your Grandchildren by Dennis Jaffe

A Wealth of Possibilities by Ellen Perry

Chapter 4 – Vision

Once the family's identity has been thoroughly articulated, then the family can begin to define its longer-term vision. Like core values, it is easy to be flippant about vision and reduce it to platitudes. In the corporate world, vision statements almost always fall victim to this.

Family visions are trickier. In one sense, they can easily fall prey to toxic positivity. Visions that define the family's success as Lake Wobegon-esque lose credibility because they feel disconnected from reality, a fact quickly pointed out by the family's skeptics. Regardless, the tendency of life to not pull its punches will remove all delusions of idyllic grandeur.

What then are the components of a well-defined family vision?

First, the family vision **must be compelling** to the individual. Individual family members are busy and have competing demands on their time. A vision should very clearly define what is in it for them.

I recognize that for some readers that sort of self-interest may sound antithetical to the sort of ethos you may be trying to cultivate in your family—commonly this ethos is centered around hard work, stewardship, and self-sacrifice. To this I would offer that such an ethos is aspirational in nature, and in time, you may see the family come around to this way of thinking.

In the interim, you need to be practical and pragmatic to get buy-in from some family members. Making the juice worth the squeeze is key. If you can get the family at the table, the desired behaviors and motivations can emerge over time.

Second, the family vision, while it cannot ignore the individual, must be collective in nature. As a rule, **people want to be a part of something bigger than themselves**. They desire to invest their lives in something that is going to make a difference. The family should not shy away from articulating a high view and where it wants to go.

Third, **the family vision should be both qualitative and quantitative**. From a qualitative perspective, it should be descriptive of the experience that you are trying to develop. What does it really look and feel like to be a part of the family? How will you all conduct yourselves culturally to support, grow, and develop one another?

At the same time, there should be a quantitative dimension. A business can point to revenue, growth rates, or shareholder returns as instrumental elements of realizing a successful vision. While family enterprise success is different, you can still come up with quantitative measures that tell you you're on the right track.

Consider things like participation rates in family meetings, participation on family committees, number of family members who have started businesses, and number of family members completing college, with advanced degrees. With a little thought you can develop metrics that are in line with the vision.

Fourth, **the vision must be attainable.** Over a reasonable length of time, let's say ten or fifteen years, a material amount of the vision could actually come to pass. If it is too lofty and feels too utopian, it will become discouraging.

Fifth, **the vision must be adaptable**. The sands of time will cause the family to evolve and change. The vision should be able to adapt to changing circumstances and times. If you realize parts of the vision more quickly than planned, you should be able to extend or grow upon the ideas.

Sixth, **the vision must be expansive.** The task ahead must be large and broad enough that all family members can envision a place where they are able to contribute. If it is too narrow, only those with the perceived level of expertise required will volunteer or be selected to contribute.

The vision must involve a broad group of subject matter areas to draw in engagement. It should also require skills that the family does not have yet—opportunities for further learning or places where new arrivals to the family (rising generations and in-laws) can step up and contribute.

Finally, the vision must be democratically developed. Command and control decision-making may work in building a great fortune, but it is antithetical to building a great family.

For the vision to be shared by all, it must be developed by all. The family's senior leader must shift over time to the role of wise advisor and find ways to support the group as they develop the vision. If there is a particular course of action that the leader feels is imperative, they must learn the delicate art of soft power and influence.

Suggested Reading:

The Life We're Looking For: Reclaiming Relationship in a Technological World by Andy Crouch

The Culture Code: The Secrets of Highly Successful Groups by Daniel Coyle

The Myth of the Silver Spoon: Navigating Family Wealth and Creating an Impactful Life by Kristin Keffeler

Chapter 5 – Strategy

With the family's identity and vision articulated, a more specific plan or strategy can be developed. As Michael Porter noted in his 1996 *Harvard Business Review* article "What is Strategy?", "Competitive strategy is about being different. It means deliberately choosing a different set of activities to deliver a unique mix of value."

What this means then is that there may be many possible paths to realizing the vision of the family. Strategy is about choosing which one to take; that is, choosing *to do* certain things should mean that you are not choosing to do others. Doing everything is not strategic.

Activities, as highlighted in the Porter quote above, are the specific actions that the family will take. There is a smorgasbord of potential activities that a family could choose. For example, families may have annual get-togethers, a college scholarship program, a speaker series, an investment fund, a family business, a family foundation, shared vacation properties and so on.

Here it is important to pause briefly and discuss the concept of being "mutually exclusive and collectively exhaustive" (MECE), a concept developed and promoted by the consulting firm McKinsey & Company. When encountering something complex, one way to make sense of it is to break it down into its component parts. Similarly, one way to organize a big group of data is to group it into smaller, similar groups.

When creating these subgroups, McKinsey and others recommend that the goal is to push for things that are MECE—meaning categories that are separate (i.e., exclusive of one another) and describe all possible options (collectively exhaustive).

Now back to the possible activities of the family. At the core, the simplest way to describe the purpose of a family enterprise is growth. Within that overarching purpose though, **there are three mutually exclusive, collectively exhaustive categories of activities** that families can engage in to grow. Namely, families can grow the family, grow their financial assets, and grow their communities. Anything else that families choose to engage in is ultimately in service to one of these three goals.

Do not be confused by bigger, broader lists of potential purposes or activities for a family enterprise. If you consider what they are outlining, I believe you will find that they simplify down to these three categories. We will now consider each in order.

Category 1: Grow the Family

Activities that support the growth of the family do so by developing the human capital of the family and strengthening its capabilities. Generally, growing the family has three primary goals.

First, build family culture. The family should be taking its work in identity (purpose and values) along with its vision and sharing those within the broader family. Doing so helps to define and build a unique family culture. A key part of this work is family storytelling. Consider the work of Robin Fivush et al. in demonstrating the tremendous importance of storytelling in the life of the family. Rites of passage likely also fit here. All the great tribes of history have had manners and mechanisms to recognize major life milestones such as coming of age, marriage, and elderhood.

Second, growing the family by building family continuity. Continuity means that the family has determined how best to continue to stay relationally engaged. Continuity is best supported in three primary ways. *Firstly, by spending time together.* Families should figure out how to be involved in each other's lives. For many families, this takes the format of an annual meeting of the broader group each year. Regardless of format, there needs to be some degree of familiarity.

Secondly, *continuity is built by education*. Each generation of the family will need to learn and grow the capabilities of the family. They will need to learn the skills required for their life stage and level of contribution within the family. They will need to learn new skills so that the family is ready to take on new challenges.

Thirdly, *continuity is built by communication*. Communication about key family issues should be regular and transparent. It should be two-way—communication is not one directed. There should be an opportunity for response and feedback.

Finally, in growing the family, work should be done to deal sensibly with family conflict. Some family conflict can be avoided through appropriate policy development. Many hot-button issues can be headed off at the proverbial pass by considering key policies around family employment, compensation levels, and board eligibility with thoughtful policies.

Conflict can be mitigated through education and other capabilities development to ensure that people "fight fair." It can be managed by working to coordinate the correct venue so that specific grievance airing does not derail the work of the family when it is together. Elders of the family can help facilitate reconciliation efforts as needed.

Category 2: Grow the Assets

Growing financial assets is a weighty concern for families. For some, it was the creation of the financial assets that prompted the shift in mindset to thinking multi-generationally. For others, the growth of the financial assets further enhances the ability of the family to realize its long-term vision. As such, the financial assets will need to grow and perform over time for the family to continue.

Yet, it is important to not let the tail wag the dog. The gravitas of financial decision-making far too often results in financial conversations dominating the dialogue within families. Take caution to keep the vision firmly in mind and see the assets as an instrumental means, not the be-all and end-all.

There are a few strategic considerations that are important to keep in mind. First, growing the assets will include both a liability management element, as well as a growth one. Liabilities may be a traditional liability such as debt. But more common are liabilities related to income taxes and estate planning. These two sides of the same coin—that is, taxes—will require significant expertise and due attention to manage.

Second, while this is necessary, it is not sufficient to grow the assets of the family well. Having appropriate defense is essential to any winning sports team, but ultimately it is offense that must be on the board. I have written at some length about the key strategic questions that must be reckoned with in thinking about how the assets can grow. These articles are accessible at davidcwellsjr.com/articles.

I will highlight a few critical themes below regarding the growth of family assets.

First—families face an exceptionally high hurdle rate for their investments. Taxes, fees, and inflation are sizable hurdles for any investor. Combined with the desire of the family to utilize the assets (i.e., distributions) and the fact that wealthy families tend to grow at an exceptional rate, this means that families will likely need to compound their assets at close to 10 percent annualized in order for the family's per capita wealth to keep pace with the family over time.

Second—the only real variable that the family can control is its distribution rate. What percentage of the assets are available to family members for spending purposes is a critical input into developing a portfolio strategy. This percentage must be developed collaboratively and thoughtfully as it is fertile ground for significant family conflict.

Third—they must be clear about what the purpose of the wealth is. If the wealth becomes the "entrée" rather than a side dish, each generation may not develop their own professional competencies to the point that they can support themselves financially. If the wealth of the family must support the family in its entirety for all its financial needs, this will limit the ability of the assets to continue to grow.

We have referred to this dynamic as Creating a Wealth Surplus to Pass to Future Generations. This surplus creates a buffer that allows the assets to grow fast enough to keep up with the exceptional growth of the family over time, though admittedly this will be exceptionally challenging in the long run.

Figure 3 – Family Wealth Surplus Illustrated

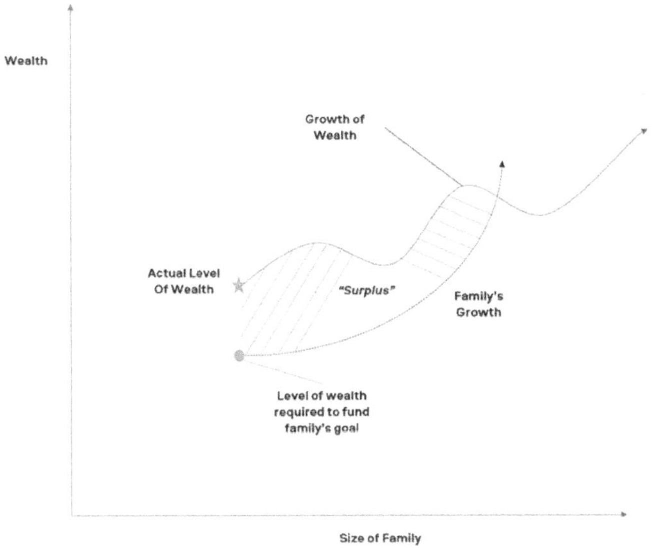

[Chart showing Wealth on vertical axis and Size of Family on horizontal axis, with curves indicating "Growth of Wealth," "Family's Growth," "Actual Level Of Wealth," "Level of wealth required to fund family's goal," and a shaded "Surplus" region between the curves.]

Source: Author

With all this in mind, the family can turn to portfolio design and construction. Here are some key strategic considerations to keep in mind while shaping an investment program:

- Families have a structural advantage to investing—namely, their long-time horizon.
- But they must be sober-minded about their business holdings and beware of treating a family business as an "heirloom asset."
- If there is buy-in, the family can look at designing their investment portfolios in a way that looks different than the consensus "market" portfolio available by third-party firms. Done well, this can help the portfolio generate attractive returns.
- Because families have owned, operated, and built businesses in the past, there is a lot of attraction to the idea of buying additional businesses. But families should exercise caution when entering the wildly competitive market for buying businesses.
- In addition to buying businesses, the family should also consider entrepreneurial ventures. But they should recognize that entrepreneurship while resource-rich is different than when resource-constrained and should take caution.

- Most likely, the family will utilize outside resources for this work. This may be a third-party firm hired to manage assets or outside talent hired to work directly for the family. The financial market is complicated, and families should consider the key differential dimensions between providers. Good investment talent is expensive and incentives must be carefully calibrated. But good investment advice can deliver significant value above its cost—so do not be penny-wise but pound-foolish.

Goal 3: Grow the Community

To this point, we have been focused only internally on the family itself. In this final category, we shift the focus outward. Growing the community is known by many names, from philanthropy to social responsibility. The dynamic here is that no family exists in a vacuum. The family, as an organic entity like a tree, sits within an ecosystem that provides resources to the family in the form of business opportunities, employees, educational institutions, houses of worship, and so on.

Just as a tree takes in those resources to live and grow, so to the tree releases oxygen back into the ecosystem. Families that are too insular may be tempted to forget about this ecosystem dynamic that contributes to their success. **As a part of the system, the family will need to return value to the system**.

While that sentiment may feel a bit like balancing karma, it is important to note the act of giving back has been well-documented to be massively beneficial to the family itself.

Developing a philanthropic strategy is at a higher level than selecting specific grantees. **To start, the family should clarify what the purpose of the family's giving is.** For some families, giving is about supporting the communities in which they have business operations. For others, philanthropy is highly focused on remedying specific social ills.

It could be a great place for emerging generations in the family to learn how to make financial decisions. It could be a place where the family can continue to work together after the sale of the business. Or for some families, collective giving is a way to show support for family members by providing funds to match or target specific areas of passion for individual family members.

There are a host of possible reasons why a family may be gathered to give; regardless, it is vitally important to define the goal lest you blend purposes and only achieve mediocrity. Each of the possibilities mentioned above, which are by no means exhaustive, could prove to be compelling for the family. But for it to be so, there must be clarity for the family about this goal. Like the values and vision dimension discussed above, philanthropy can be emotionally loaded as it hits very close to home around the causes and issues that family members care the most about.

Once the overall rationale is in place, it becomes possible to consider specific approaches. Do you fund capital projects only? Operating expenses? Create endowments? What program areas are important? How open are you to philanthropic risk—does an organization need to be well established or are you willing to invest in a new organization with a novel theory of change?

Who develops the strategy?

Across the three main categories, there are many possibilities that surface. So, who comes up with all this strategic thinking? Remember from the beginning of this section that strategy is about choices of activities. It is inherently self-limiting—by choosing to do some things, you must also choose not to do others.

Strategic thinking begins with the resources that are available to the family. The family's identity, capabilities and assets are the essential resources that the family can deploy. As the strategy takes shape, it must be constantly validated against the vision of the family.

Growing the family, the assets and the community are best thought of as instrumental ends, not ultimate ones. What this means is that these actions are in service to a greater whole. The family chooses to engage in activities that develop the family—education, regular gatherings, and so on—because they believe that those actions will ultimately contribute to the realization of the family's vision for building a family enterprise together.

As you can surmise, given the highly integrated nature between specific activities and long-term vision, the family must be closely involved in the process of crafting strategy. Only they will be able to determine whether an expressed idea feels aligned with the heart of their long-term goals.

Yet, while the family should be involved in this process, at the strategic level, **all thinking must be tested against reality to determine feasibility.** The best ideas in the world that are not actually doable are of no use to the family. As such, there will need to be subject matter experts engaged in conjunction with the family at this stage. These could be consultants who are engaged only on a temporary basis, an in-house team that will be tasked with bringing all this to fruition, or a third-party firm, such as a multi-family office, that will be intimately involved with the family's affairs.

Let's get more specific. For example, what exactly does a well-articulated strategy for growing the family, assets, and community look like? It is an important question, but the answer must unfortunately remain somewhat vague. Ultimately, strategy should be descriptive but not a playbook. You can tell an architect that you want a house of a certain size and in a certain style. But no architect wants an architect for a client.

To best leverage the team/group/people involved in the execution, you want to leave the specifics of implementation somewhat open-ended. This allows their individual creativity and expertise to emerge. The net result of this will be a more engaged team (from doing more interesting work) and a better outcome because you have not artificially constrained them in their work. The family is best then served by taking each of the three focus areas and beginning to articulate specific goals and critical parameters.

In addition, careful consideration should be given to what metrics should be tracked to tell the family that they are on the right path. Certainly, metrics have a degree of danger embedded—as Goodhart's law so eloquently states, "When a measure becomes a target, it ceases to be a good measure."

But given that the family's vision may have significantly qualitative dimensions, it is important to give careful consideration as to how you will know if you are on the right track. The family's generational time horizon provides the flexibility to allow something to develop over time. However, a paradox arises when one is overly patient with a course of action that might lead down the wrong path or chasing after irrelevant distractions while pursuing the long-term vision.

Suggested Reading:

Family Capital by Greg Curtis

Harvard Business Review Family Business Handbook: How to Build and Sustain a Successful, Enduring Enterprise by Baron and Lachenauer

The Art of Gathering: How We Meet and Why It Matters by Priya Parker

Give Smart by Tierney and Fleishman

Creating Great Choices: A Leader's Guide to Integrative Thinking by Roger Martin

Chapter 6 – Implementation

With a vision in place and a clear strategy in mind, it is possible to begin doing the work. Implementation of the strategic plan can be straightforward as some elements of the strategic plan may have known playbooks.

For example, to grow the assets, we know that the tax liabilities of the family must be thoughtfully addressed in a timely fashion. Trained and competent professionals stand willing and able to help the family navigate the vagaries of the tax code.

For other parts of the strategic plan, **the family will need to try several different possible answers to see which is the correct solution to the problem at hand.** The right people to attempt this endeavor may not be readily apparent. Some of the roles necessary to serve a family well do not occur naturally in the job market. As such, it may be necessary to hire talent with certain skills that may require additional training to accomplish the specific goal.

As highlighted in chapter 2, the complexity of wealthy families tends to explode into being and then only continue to grow. Managing this complexity, while simultaneously executing on strategic priorities, is of critical importance.

Part and parcel of this is the very real dynamic that unlike the original "business" of the family, the family itself may be unable, unqualified, or unwilling to participate in delivering the "work" required at this stage.

So, into this potential service gap steps the organization known as the "family office." The term family office remains somewhat nebulous. The financial services industry has translated the term family office into a marketing buzzword with numerous potential interpretations.

Regardless, **the family office is the group that is tasked with bringing the family's strategic vision to life.** It is easy to see the family office as only an individual or team focused on execution, but that would be a limiting view.

Rather, it is important for the family to recognize that the family office itself is a unique organization that is supported by the family and exists to serve the family, but is ultimately separate from the family. As a distinct organization, the office will create livelihoods for the employees of the office. The office team will support the office, who will in turn support the family office.

The same is true of the office. The family benefits from the dedication and support of this group. The group benefits from a thoughtful group of clients, potential long tenure of employment, access to unique investment opportunities, and other benefits.

Importantly, many of these dynamics are true whether it is an in-house, single-family office with only a single family for a client or a multi-family office. The lines between the two are quite blurry. For the oldest families, the office itself will serve multiple households, so it is in fact a multi-family office.

So, while we have been discussing the Strategic Action Model for family enterprise purely from the perspective of the family itself, there is a parallel series of steps that the family office is taking that mirror the work the family is doing. The family office too must define its identity. It must see how the family's vision intersects with its own. Then it must take the vision and cocreate the strategies with the family to bring them to life.

And like any business, these steps do not occur in a vacuum. While a third-party firm goes to the market to find validation for its work to define itself and develop a service model, the family office does all of this work in concert with the family. This process is something akin to jazz music. The family plays a riff, followed by the family office. The family can listen and respond, to which the office must follow along and adapt.

If either side is out of step or sync with the other, what is left is a cacophony. Families and their offices see this with things like low customer service scores and high rates of turnover.

The specifics of designing a family office and how this process works has many moving pieces and parts. That is worth a separate book in its own right. In the interim, I will offer that family offices have five key considerations to wrestle with. The well-managed office will answer:

- **What will we do?** How does the office determine its service offering? Where does the family fit?
- **Who will do it?** What will the team look like? What will be done by insider's versus outsiders?
- **How will it be delivered?** With a wide range of complex and intertwined services, what is the operating model that the office will use to organize and deliver its work? How will the inevitable screw-ups be handled?
- **Will it be excellent?** How will the office manage the quality of its output? What can be standardized and what must be bespoke?
- **Is it sustainable?** Is there an economic model that supports the work to be done?

Suggested Reading:

The Family Office: A Comprehensive Guide by William Woodson and Edward Marshall

Excellence Wins by Horst Schulze

What It Takes: Seven Secrets of Success from the World's Greatest Professional Firms by Charles Ellis

Chapter 7 – Governance

So where are we at this point? There is an articulated and shared sense of family identity. A vision has been cast of what the family is attempting to do by staying relationally engaged. In support of that vision, specific choices have been made to define the strategy and its activities for the family to continue to grow the family, the assets, and its community. All these great ideas have not remained on a whiteboard, they are being brought to life through a family office-like entity tasked with their implementation.

As you can see, a lot has been set in motion to design this system that supports the family. The only final element remaining is governance—which helps keep the whole process on track and heading in the right direction.

Good governance is almost unanimously agreed to be of great importance, yet it remains a challenge to implement, and candidly even challenging to talk about. Governance and its complement, government, are topics that have been discussed since ancient times.

At its core, there is a tension that is embedded in the very concept of organizational governance. In the corporate world (and thereby through legal structures), governance is implemented to address the problem of agency. The principal-agent problem describes the fact that for many organizations, those in charge are not the owners.

As a result, there is a potential conflict of interest where the agent could take steps to benefit him or herself at the expense of the owner. Boards of directors are put into place to address this dynamic by overseeing and raising appropriate guardrails.

And not surprisingly, like the child who bemoans being slowed in their efforts to go play outside by a parent urging them to put on a jacket or shoes, the agent, who may in fact be entirely well meaning, can see this sort of governance as an actual hinderance to their work. Perhaps you have driven a go-cart or golf cart and been frustrated by the presence of a "governor" on your ability to go as fast as you wish.

And yes, while all boards have fiduciary matters that they must attend to, **there is a higher, nobler purpose of governance that is much more productive**. The board can become the critical thought partner to the management team in considering if the organizational strategy, its execution, and subsequent results are working as they should, tracking to long-term goals, and aware of and prepared for change that is coming. Governance of a family enterprise is no different.

Let's acknowledge at the outset that the idea of governance and family is awkward. We most commonly do not think about social systems as needing governance. There is no "president" or chairman when I get together with my friends, and I would guess the same is true for you. The emergence of governance marks the shift of the family from a purely social system into an organizational one.

Good governance helps the enterprise understand how it is doing and if it is progressing toward its stated vision.

So where does governance fit in the action model we have been articulating? I would argue that governance sits in four places—governance will be needed in overseeing each of the growth activities—growing the family, assets, and community, and then some sort of system-wide governance that oversees the whole thing. This could be as many as four separate boards of directors/advisory boards.

Each of the activities is complicated enough that there will be meaningful work for a governance entity to do. But then there must also be an overarching entity that considers the health of the whole system—lest it fall prey to the old analogy of a zebra being a horse designed by committee.

Traditionally governance in the family enterprise was based on looking at the three circles diagram and assuming that each circle—family, business, and ownership needed its own governance entity. While that sounds good in theory, in my experience, it has rarely been the case.

Governance should be seated where it can address a piece of the workstream of the enterprise. There must be enough to oversee, or else the governance will feel ineffective. But its mandate should not be so large as to make it impossible to manage. With that in mind, there are a few places where governance immediately jumps out as important.

First, under the "grow the family" workstream, there will most likely need to be a family-focused governance entity created. This entity is most often referred to as a family council. Family councils traditionally oversee the human capital and capability development of the family. Most commonly this is through development of family culture (stories, rites of passage, values), family continuity (relationship development, family gatherings, and conflict management (including communication).

Second, the family foundation or philanthropic entity may be required to have a board or group of trustees from a legal/regulatory perspective. The functional reality may be quite different. For many family foundations, the work of its board is just an extension of the family council or sometimes the work of the family council.

Finally, the "grow the assets" workstream. If a family business remains, it may have its own governance entity. Post-liquidity event families may have an investment committee overseeing the investment activities.

So, who governs the family office? In some families, the family office is the business entity and so it gets treated under the "grow the assets" workstream. Because the office serves as the implementor of a large portion of the strategic plan, it is important to make sure that its governance is representative of all the constituents who are dependent on its activities.

In addition to these "functional" level governance entities that oversee a particular part of the activity stream of the family enterprise (grow the family, grow the assets, grow the community), there will likely need to be some macro-level body that considers the whole and not just the parts. This steering group serves a vital role in the coordination of activities.

Also, for matters like communication and education that are needed parts of the family enterprise, but will likely be engaged in by multiple entities, there should be a single point of consolidation to discuss such matters. This entity should likely also include senior leadership of the family office whose team will be tasked with "doing" large portions of identified work.

Chapter 8 – Concluding Matters

Figure 2 – The Strategic Action Model ("SAM")

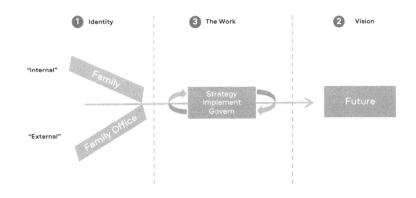

We are nearing the end of our discussion of the SAM. This is hopefully just the end of the beginning. Each of the dimensions we discussed could be probed in much greater depth—and in fact, there are whole books that do just that.

That was not our task here. One of my favorite models is the 80/20 rule or the Pareto principle. The rule states that 80 percent of the consequences arise from 20 percent of the causes. This sort of thinking is powerful when put into practice.

The SAM is designed to show you the pathway to get 80 percent of the output with 20 percent of the input. Certainly, there are additional levels of understanding and input that will be needed.

But, as a starting place, having a clear framework to begin from provides a much-needed lightening of the cognitive load. Take the SAM with you as you read, meet other families, attend conferences, and so on. What you will hear will hopefully provide you with a better understanding of how and why a given family's actions fit into their model, and if it might work in yours.

How does this work in practice? Most commonly, families are textbook examples of "building the plane while flying it." While the SAM is laid out in a somewhat linear fashion, the reality is that, most likely, families are working across all its various parts simultaneously.

It is worth a word of caution that the work of identity should be begun as quickly as possible, and toward the earlier end. If we have learned nothing else from all the Matt Damon / Jason Bourne films about the spy suffering from amnesia, it is that it is quite hard to do anything if you do not know who you are. Families are no different.

This work is never really done. As the family progresses toward its vision, it should regularly evaluate its progress and the family itself and determine what has changed or might need to change. The work is not static by any means but happens in a dynamic world. The family should be ready to shift and respond as required by changing circumstances.

One question you may be asking is how many people are needed to do this? This is one place where I hope to be encouraging. There are many families who are later in generations with hundreds of family members and billions of dollars of financial resources. Seeing and hearing about their robust family enterprise structures can be simultaneously inspiring, but also intimidating. It seems far easier to build out all these various entities when there is a large group of people from which to draw.

The reality is that the core of the family enterprise more than anything is the culture itself. That is why the SAM begins with identity and vision. These cultural markers are far more important in marking off a family enterprise that is serious about the goal of persistence for hundreds of years.

If the family can get the culture right and create a place that is welcoming and the sort of organization that the family wants to be a part of, it will likely be able to figure out the rest. The activities involved in growing the family, thoughtful giving, or even capital allocation can be done internally or with the partnership of thoughtful outsiders who will happily work alongside the family.

We began in chapter 1 by encouraging the family first to consider its goals and intentions for moving wealth to future generations. People would do well to carefully consider whether they are serious about the task of building a legacy family / family enterprise.

Part and parcel of this choice is understanding whether the family wants to be engaged in a collective act or not. I believe there are compelling reasons why someone might choose to be part of a family such as this. But the point is that the reasons must be compelling, above and beyond a sense of guilt or obligation. Guilt may work in the beginning, but it will not be robust enough for the family to persist over time.

If the family is reasonably bought in, the point is to get started. As the Chinese proverb goes, **"The best time to plant a tree was twenty years ago. The second-best time is now."**

Appendix

Over the course of this book, I have discussed various statements and documents that are worthwhile to prepare. In an effort to support those ideas, I have drafted a series of example statements for a hypothetical Smith family to show what each could look like.

Purpose Statement

Today, the Smith families consists of 3 living generations - G1 (mom and dad), G2 (siblings and their spouses), and G3 (grandchildren). We desire to build a family that will persist for seven generations (~150 years), which is our aspirational target. By G7, no present living generation will be around. If we are successful in keeping the family together, it means that our purpose, values, and vision have been brought to life in such a way that despite the family being entirely 'new,' they have chosen this path for themselves.

We believe that our family is and can continue to be a powerful source of identity, continuity, and opportunity for current and future generations. In a world marked by change and uncertainty, we believe that the support, love, and affection of family will greatly enhance the lives of future family members and offer them the greatest chances to live lives of meaning and happiness.

Values

While there are many values and virtues that are important to the family and its members, the following four are the most resonate with our family and story.

Hard Work - We believe each family member has abilities and talents that are best used in working hard for the benefit of others.

Integrity - We are the people that we say we are. Our word and character are a sacred trust.

Respect - We treat others and ourselves with great dignity.

Wisdom – While we are not scared to be innovative, we are also not willing to be foolish. We gather insight from others, and we contemplate our actions carefully.

Vision statement

In one generation, if we are successfully marching towards our seven-generation goal, we believe the following will be true:

Our family is a place of warmth and support. Family members enjoy one another and want to spend time together. We are each other's greatest cheerleaders.

We know that in our individual lives, we will have different experiences and make different life choices. We have developed the skills to support one another and not let differences around politics, religion, and spending choices become so dominate that the family is unable to be around one another. We aspire to lead with curiosity and not with condemnation when facing a disagreement.

We will be a group that communicates well. We abhor gossip and believe that careful candor is a practice we must all work to develop. In the same way, we aspire to be a family that is quick to forgive wrongs - especially when they are inadvertent.

We aspire to see family members making a difference in the world. While there are times and seasons for rest and restoration, we also have a responsibility to act. Where the tremendous talents of this family intersect the needs of this world, we have an opportunity to find a way to use our gifts, talents, and abilities for the betterment of the places and spaces we call home. This is a broad mandate and includes more than just our 'professional careers.'

We understand that the modern world is exceptionally busy, and our family members' lives are no different. If our family enterprise is successful, we believe it must successfully "compete" with other social organizations that our family members are engaged with.

To know we are heading towards this vision, we believe the following indicators are worth tracking:

Family:
- Percentage of family in attendance at family gatherings
- Education attainment by family – including degrees, professional certifications, and vocational training
- Annual survey of family members on Net Promoter Score

Financial Assets:
- Rate of return vs. benchmark and historically
- Rate of return vs. targeted growth rate
- Percentage of capital base generated from new ventures over the past 5 / 10 / 20 years

Community:
- Percentage of the family members actively involved in volunteering or serving on non-profit boards
- Dollar amounts given annually and cumulatively since inception
- Hours volunteered annually and cumulatively since inception

Family Enterprise Strategy

Grow the Family

For us to be successful, we believe that in addition to growing our family assets, the family must grow as well. While we look forward to welcoming in-laws and children, the existing family will need to continue to grow its own capabilities.

To support this growth, we recommend that the financial assets produce a distribution of 0.5% annually to invest in family causes. We believe those funds should be used in the following ways:

1) Family gathering - Each year the family needs to be spending time together. We will gather for a fun, casual, relationship building time for one week each summer. The expenses for this trip will be covered by the family enterprise. The goal for this time is relationship building, not content delivery. Accommodations for the trip should be of a nice enough degree to be attractive to attend, but not necessarily luxurious, as that is not the purpose of the trip.

2) Education - We know that if our family and its members are to be successful, we all will need to continue to grow our knowledge and understanding. To that end, we are establishing an annual personal development budget of $2,500 per adult family member. These funds can be used to attend classes, work with executive coaches, etc. Unspent funds may be carried over year to year to an amount not to exceed $10,000.

3) Communication - Communication is vitally important and exceptionally difficult. To that end, we will take the following steps. The family will have one additional weekend gathering per year. The gathering will be facilitated by a paid family enterprise consultant. The family council, if established, or a small multi-generational steering group, will work with the consultant to shape the content and agenda of this time. Business/financial specific updates will be provided twice per year and may be delivered virtually or in another convenient fashion.

4) Stories - The history and stories of our family are part of what make us great. As each generations ages, we will work to capture key stories of the family on video.

5) Entrepreneurship - Starting new ventures and the creation of new value have been seminal to the on-going success of the family. While our financial assets may support the growth of new ventures through investments in venture capital, we believe the family must continue to build the muscle of new venture development.

As part of our regular gatherings, we will invite local entrepreneurs (both creators of businesses as well as non-profits) to come and speak. We will encourage our young family members to take entrepreneurship courses at school. We will look to leverage Babson College's entrepreneurship in family enterprise program.

Grow Our Financial Assets

To support our purpose and the achievement of our vision, we know and understand that financial assets will be necessary resources, but not ultimately sufficient.

We believe that financial assets are the 'dessert, not the entrée' for family members. We believe every family member should pursue financial self-sufficiency. The ability to take care of oneself is a vital part of maturation and is highly supportive of living a purposeful and happy life.

At the same time, the financial assets of the family should be used as a blessing in the lives of family members - to create opportunities, support individual growth, encourage family relationships, etc.

To that end, the family has set a target for a 1.5% annual distribution of assets that should be generated by the financial assets of the family. We have developed this distribution rate in conjunction with our advisors to balance this rate with our longer-term goals, as well as opportunities available for return in the financial markets.

Grow Our Communities

As our family and its wealth has grown, it has been supported greatly by our local community. The employees of our original family business were instrumental in its growth. In recognition of that, the family has always worked to support local causes that helped improve the communities we call home.

Moreover, we know that the power of financial wealth that exceeds individual needs and wants has the potential to lead to us to become excessively self-focused and less aware of others. As such, both for the good done in our communities and the good done in our hearts, we want to be a family known for its charitable engagement in the community.

Through our grant making, we wish to support causes that are in alignment with our core values. We also believe that by giving together, we will grow a more thoughtful and intentional family through the shared opportunity for multiple generations to be involved in our charitable work.

About The Author

David is a Managing Director at Greycourt & Co, Inc. Prior to joining Greycourt in 2023, David founded Family Capital Strategy, a strategy consultancy for family offices in 2019. Previously, David was a partner at an asset management firm in Nashville after spending many years as a fundamental investor and analyst.

David has and continues to serve in a broad range of governance roles. Currently, he serves as Chair of the Board for a midwestern Private Trust Company, board member for a Southeastern Private Trust Company, and an Investment Committee Member for a Foundation. He is also on the Board of 21/64, a national practice advising family philanthropies.

He is the author of **When Anything is Possible: Wealth and the Art of Strategic Living**. He lives in Nashville, TN.

You can reach him at davidcwellsjr.com and at info@davidcwellsjr.com

Made in United States
Orlando, FL
10 December 2023

39925098R00046